Friend of Heraclitus

Also by Patricia Beer from Carcanet

Collected Poems
Moon's Ottery

PATRICIA BEER
Friend of Heraclitus

CARCANET

First published in in 1993 by
Carcanet Press Limited
208-212 Corn Exchange Buildings
Manchester M4 3BQ

A CIP catalogue record for this book
is available from the British Library.
ISBN 1 85754 026 3

The publisher acknowledges financial assistance
from the Arts Council of Great Britain.

Set in 10½pt Sabon by Bryan Williamson, Frome, Somerset
Printed and bound in England by SRP Ltd, Exeter

For Miranda Duncker

Acknowledgements

Some of these poems first appeared in the following
programmes and publications, to whose producers
and editors thanks are due: BBC Radio 3, BBC Radio 4,
A Garland for Stephen Spender (arranged by
Barry Humphries), *John Bunyan and His England*
(eds. W.R. Owens, Anne Laurence and Stuart Sim),
Life by Other Means (ed. Jacqueline Sims),
London Review of Books, Poetry Book Society
Anthologies, *PN Review*, the *Sunday Times*,
The Tablet.

Contents

Observations

Friend of Heraclitus

Still are thy pleasant voices, thy nightingales, awake
For death he taketh all away but them he cannot take.
WILLIAM CORY

For one thing I do not believe in nightingales.
They were thought up by the deaf for the deaf.
The number of times I have walked away
From the sound of my own feet
Into the wood where the birds were said to foregather
And heard nothing but the night air growing cold:
Just as I lost a world-famous eclipse
In a purely local rainstorm
And narrowly missed
The great comet as it slid back into the sky
For the next hundred years.
Nightingales.

Certainly I hear yours now, sleepless
Before dawn brings life back to the curtains.

But dear Heraclitus, you must not depend on me
Or my compeers, to keep even one of them
Singing and hearty for ever, or for long.
Death *can* take away all your nightingales,
And will do. When he takes our heads.

The Voice

When God took my aunt's baby boy, a merciful neighbour
Gave her a parrot. She could not have afforded one
But now bought a new cage as brilliant as the bird,
And turned her back on the idea of other babies.

He looked unlikely. In her house his scarlet feathers
Stuck out like a jungle, though his blue ones blended
With the local pottery which carried messages
Like 'Du ee help yerself to crame, me handsome.'

He said nothing when he arrived, not a quotation
From pet-shop gossip or a sailor's oath, no sound
From someone's home: the telephone or car-door slamming,
And none from his: tom-tom, war-cry or wild beast roaring.

He came from silence but was ready to become noise.
My aunt taught him nursery rhymes morning after morning.
He learnt Miss Muffett, Jack and Jill, Little Jack Horner,
Including her jokes; she used to say turds and whey.

A genuine Devon accent is not easy. Actors
Cannot do it. He could though. In his court clothes
He sounded like a farmer, as her son might have.
He sounded like our family. He fitted in.

Years went by. We came and went. A day or two
Before he died, he got confused, and muddled up
His rhymes. Jack Horner ate his pail of water.
The spider said what a good boy he was. I wept.

He had never seemed puzzled by the bizarre events
He spoke of. But that last day he turned his head towards us
With the bewilderment of death upon him. Said
'Broke his crown' and 'Christmas pie'. And tumbled after.

My aunt died the next winter, widowed, childless, pitied
And patronised. I cannot summon up her voice at all.
She would not have expected it to be remembered
After so long. But I can still hear his.

Guillotine, 1989

In nineteen-eighty-nine we recall a revolution.
From those street-lamps you could not hang anybody
Yet mobs dance under them. World leaders talk
Revolution. Hermits fantasise. The word is in the air.

Here in the country it is raining. Did they use
The guillotine when it was raining? Would it work?
Certainly all that knitting would get wet, and cold drops
Strike the neckbones before the slanting blade did.

I am trying to write. In the next room
My husband cuts articles from his professional
Magazines. I hear the sound of beheading, the sound
Of the guillotine. I listen. It is lifelike:

Preliminary footsteps on the scaffold. A dreadful pause
For organization and correct placing. The squeal
Of weight being pulled up, the rumble of weight descending,
The blow, and then unidentifiable noises.

It lasts for an hour. How many humans were despatched
In that time? Dickens would have worked it out.
I join my husband. He stands there innocently
Holding a piece of paper clean cut.

A mutilated journal lies on the table, bright
Still with diagrams and charts and potential.
He will tidy it away later. Meanwhile in his hand
The airy cutting throbs as his blood beats.

Regency Girls Dancing

The feathers in our hair
Reach up like stalagmites
Towards the descending crystals
Of the chandeliers.

Though neither is growing
It seems the two might meet
In this bright cave.
The dance has not yet begun
But we are in place.

The music strikes and we leap.
Our feathers bob and bounce
In an earthquake.

The piercing stalactites
Swing round in search of us
To pick our feathers out.

Long After Waterloo

This soldier from his grave declares
That he was nothing but his wars.
His soul was made out of camp-fires.

His tombstone does not say he fought
Simply that he was present at —
And then the battle's name and date.

His name is small, the battle's large.
He was the bayonet and the dirge.
He was the chinstrap and the charge.

A dozen yew trees further on
The memory of his name has gone.
It lingered somewhere with his son.

This way he has become a street,
A bridge, a station, the defeat
That any overlord could meet.

The tombstone is his state of mind.
Now as the evening sun comes round
Something is rising from the ground:

The sweet smell of humility?
For he was present on that day
Yet what he did he does not say.

Channel Tunnel

Lands parted since the ice age
Can ignore the sea again
Now that a long dry hall
Leads from one language to another.

The tunnellers were as far from home
As Crusaders, as tough and hard-hatted.
Some died
And were hoisted up
To the topsoil of the globe.

When the work was done
The rest moved on
Their dead following slowly.

All had struggled with earth and stone
But none could settle like farmers.

They had staved off the sea
But the sea is still as strong as Atlas
And with flexible back and arms
Supports shipping and storms.

Statues

We are the first to go
In public uprisings,
They say. That is not true.
Other images sow

And reap revolution.
Lorries will bear us off
But not as first or last.
It is transmigration.

Our heads are so weighty
The rope round our throats
Keeps us horizontal
In air. We fall, mighty.

They lower us, long coats
Hanging sideways, into
Our shadows that reach out;
Into those seemly crates.

They do not break us; theirs
Is old rage. A dog trots
Over us, lifts his leg
High but nobody jeers.

Though we were murderers,
Our hands in our pockets,
For decades we have stood
Where no criminal stirs.

Do we have one mourner
As the lorries move? We
Seek a new public square,
A different street corner.

Cockcrow

Upright at five o'clock on an August morning
We carry light luggage out of the house.
With heavy cases our children stoop.
Their children are winged
With small bright backpacks.

The sky is a shop window before opening-time,
Goods shadowy as trees. But in a back room
And spreading, the light will soon come on.

We breathe cautiously in the untried air,
Talk warily at the centre of six fields.

And then comes cockcrow, swaggering up
Out of the valley. The invisible bird
Plumes himself. He was the one chosen
To nail good terrified Peter. He conquers
The dark with flying colours.

We wave our dear children and theirs
Into the growing light. We are old
And sleep late after bad nights.
We shall not hear the conquistador again
Till they visit us in another season
Travelling up the valley like cockcrow.

Grave Doubts

Peace to Lord Hamlet, I have never heard
Gravediggers talking. Before the funeral
You see them from a distance, usually
In mist, moving eloquently
But without speech in a pas de deux.

On that day when the clergyman's voice
Had had its say and gone back into its box,
In the silence of people turning to go home
And the receding mutter of an empty
Hearse, the gravediggers closed in.

Taciturn caterers, they stared down at the coffin
Spread out on its base of earth. Mutely
They sandwiched it in soil. And then they went
Away to wash their hands of it. I thought
That they would never cross my path again.

Many years later, the only relation left,
I came in search of the plot and could not find it.
The manager, in her steamy little hut,
Explained to me that the grave was 'unpurchased'.
'A *pauper's* grave?' 'That's what they used to say.'

I asked her what might happen now. She said
The gravediggers could come back without a word
To me or anybody else, remove
The contents, add to it, or anything.
She liked telling me that. I purchased it.

A crested document arrived this morning
And I became, as in the childhood chapters
Of some second-rate autobiography,
The proud possessor of. Not of a bicycle
Not of a pony or a doll's house. Of a grave.

He was a distant cousin, but I am glad
To have bought one respectable old man
From the gravediggers. They deafened him once.
Now he will hold his peace in the deadpan dark
And will not hear spade voices ever again.

E.T. *Phone Home.*

E.T. looked like my cousin
Who looked like many things wise
And wonderful: certain dreams,
Ancient jars in museums,
Fetishes with level eyes
And their native soil still on.

I was a child. I loved him
We could most peacefully play
Together. Our family
Feared the neighbours might think we
Were *all* balmy. He could say
Three or four words. One was 'Home'.

At thirteen he was taken
Away to an asylum.
For three days he wailed one word:
'Home, home, home...' Nobody heard.
Then sedated he fell dumb
Leaving the air shaken.

Soon we were told he had died.
No property, clothes or last
Words came back. But a nurse said
That he always laughed out loud
When another inmate cursed.
Those who sent him there cried.

I heard this film was coming,
Fifty years later, on TV
And watched it. Now I often see
Rainbowing up a dark sky
And heavier by one boy,
My kin, a space-ship homing.

Pharaoh's Dream

In childhood I thought of cows and dreams together
Starting from Pharaoh's dream of seven well-favoured kine
Followed by seven other kine, lean-fleshed
That did eat them up.

Joseph the farmer, dressy as Pharaoh, told him
At once that throughout his many-coloured land
Famine would succeed plenty, seven years of each.
Pharaoh wrung his smooth

Hands, not having considered such a meaning.
Literal in eastern daylight he could not see
Cows eating each other or being real danger.
I thought he was stupid.

I knew the red cows of East Devon.
Our branch-line ran through water-meadows and they
Were always getting on the track. We knew
The times of the trains

And shooed them off. Even a child could do it.
But they did not go far. Making red footprints
In the frail grass, they mooched a few yards then turned
To face the track again.

Pharaoh only dreamed of cows. In my case
They were the dreams themselves, bad dreams
That never quitted the field though you could scatter them
Simply by waking up.

Most of them left gently but one always looked round
With the death-rattle of a moo,
Swinging a bright chain of spittle, a torturer
Who planned to be back.

Beach Party

One week after the death exactly
Friends took us out
To the shadowless beach of childhood
Where every summer Saturday,
A blue flower filling the sky,
We had gone with my mother.

We found we could still play.
We yelled at the hot sand,
Screamed at the cold water.

Then a wind got up.
The corn on the cliff top
Became a whispering gallery
That boomed around the bay,
And a cloud, fat and foreign as a zeppelin,
Trundled out of some strange place.

Over the sand its shadow crept towards us
Welcome at first. I had never minded
The heat of the sun before.

As it came nearer I curled up like prey.
At my right temple it narrowed and streamed in,
The comic strip of a ghost.

All afternoon,
Pretending to be sad which they understood,
I watched the empty sand
On the other side of me.

And when the beach party got up to go,
As at all picnics everybody carried something.

Footbinding

My grandmother had a small shelf of books
Hanging in a shadow. One of them
Was Foxe's Book of Martyrs. All the rest
Were works by missionaries who had served
In China. They were handsome volumes, hard
With gold and angry colours, heavy with Empire.
I never saw her read them but she handed
Them out to me like medicine. As well
As every other heathen practice, they
Described footbinding. In their godly fashion
The missionaries revelled in the cracking
Of the maiden's bones, the consternation
Of her bloodstream, the whining of her sinews
And the two years of agony ahead.
It was far worse than Foxe's Book of Martyrs.

My mother's and her mother's feet were tiny.
Mine were thin but long and getting longer.
Would those two organise a ceremony
Where women gathered and the screaming started?
Probably not. They planned on twisting me
Into a little lady if it killed them
But definitely would not want to be
Anything but the smallest feet in town.

Nowadays I think of those girls in China
Who ran and pounced and almost flew until
The day they never pounced or ran again.
Their fledgling feet did not grow into birds.
Some of them died of gangrene. Some went mad.
But those who lived, nubile, felt like orchids.
Their family's approval smelled of jasmine
As, fluttering in silk, they married Emperors.

An aim the missionaries did not mention.

Senior Members

Senior members, writing
To the college chronicle
Give more news than they mean to.
With only one name on show
The class of 'seventeen must all
Have lost men in the fighting.

They deny they are housebound
Yet one speaks of nothing but
A dome she sees in the sun
From her west window, and one
Mentions three years running that
She is very nearly blind.

The class of 'eighty-four teach,
Do social work and teach. They
Win lacklustre prizes yet
In God's good time will fan out
Into sinners and saints. We
Shall not know how far they stretch.

The class of 'forty, my class,
Tell us (I do not write in)
They have retired but conceal
From what. Some of them reveal
How grand their husbands have been.
What odd matters they confess:

One does not use her title
Much – what *was* it? – nowadays.
One has been given a set
Of handbells. One is a hermit.
One appeared on Songs of Praise.
One has moved down to Cornwall.

But grandmothers they all are.
Children they did not conceive,
Nor could have, identify
Them like Saturn's rings. Their sky
Dims, but those they are proud of
Skip round them in the night air.

Not War

Newly shorn, the ewes are Aryan white
In our front field. This June is warm,
Almost erotic for England, and they loll
Like odalisques about the bright green farm,

But more like all those groups of Nordic maidens
Looking up in fascist interwar
Paintings at warriors who will fertilise them,
One naked maiden to each warrior.

Our ram arrived today but will not work
Until the dawn. He has his bag of paint –
Bright blue this year – already fastened on.
Alone and independent as a saint

At the top of the field, he has no war in him,
No resolution of the heroic sort,
Yet waits up there in the dark, his harness on,
Looking for day, as if at Agincourt.

A Day in the Life

Awake, for morning in the summer trees
Has brought the leafy darkness to its knees.
The east shuffles and parts to let day through.
The stars have lapsed into dead certainties.

I must start writing. That is what I do.
Time does not give me what I want it to.
The farm moves forward. Food goes through its gut.
And I am as immobile as the view.

The cows enter the back field and begin
Lowering the grass before the sheep come in.
The meadow circulates with piebald flanks,
Angel-white legs and faces black as sin.

The sun rolls round, pale as an orange peeled.
And now the chimneys crawl across the field:
Antennae, reaching for the other farms
To catch the sounds of work. My lips are sealed.

I open the back door. The kitchen light
Transforms the meadow powdery and white
To ashes. In it embers seem to glow.
I have switched on the sheep's eyes in the night.

In the five hours of darkness that remain
Bad dreams with my name on could pierce and drain
The black sloth off. Tomorrow I may sit
Here writing, catching up the farm again.

Early Work

(at the Van Gogh exhibition)

Two of the four trees have been
Moved apart so that the back
View of the woman in black
Can take up a pose between
Them. Early work. Her white hat
Shines like a child's paper boat.

Autumn browned the trees before
The sappy land could catch up.
The woman came to a stop.
She could not go anywhere
Except to some prayer meeting
For the saved. She is waiting.

Later work. Everything feels
Free now to take its own
Course. In the fields, sheaves sown
Months ago flap off like seals.
Tree trunks turn into torsos,
Bodies struggle to be trees.

Down the lane at close of day
A man, a metaphor, homes
In on us all. He comes
Purposefully, on his way
To a rally of madmen
In the asylum garden.

Pilgrims Crossing

Watch out for pilgrims crossing. Their
Good hour strikes. The messenger
From the eternal city has come
Back into time to summon them.

A dreadful master they have found
Time to be. They never owned
Much, and now these common waves
Deny them even their own graves.

All the misfortunes they have met
Were on some other man's estate.
Christian saw Apollyon
Coming across his fields at noon

Calling him in a dragon's voice
A servant. Waiting now to cross
The river, confident, they stand
On the coast of Beulah Land.

Beulah is a deathbed dream
Of what will be the heavenly home
And never was on earth: the arts,
Help in the house and beds with sheets,

No need to walk, no need to sleep,
A piece of land that they can keep.
At the riverside they glimpse these things
In the city of the King of Kings.

Ready-to-Halt has given away
His crutches. He will always be
A cripple but now very rich,
A lame man in a golden coach.

The village idiot, Feeble-mind,
Has left his moonstruck brain behind
With his protective mops and mows.
He will be needed where he goes.

They do not look for other change.
The celestial kingdom is not strange,
Simply a better-governed one,
A kindly version of their own.

They crossed the river long ago.
What happened there we cannot know.
The only man who might have said,
The man who made them up, is dead.

The trumpet and the chariot
Meant nothing much to him. He put
More value on the pilgrims' pains
And progress in this world. Grace reigns.

Poem Found in a Modern Church

I wish I knew more about this church
I wish I could get to know better
More of the people of this church
I wish the minister would preach a sermon on...
I wish the congregation would sing my favourite hymn,
Number...
I wish I had offering envelopes
I wish I could serve the church in some capacity
Such as...
I wish...

*   *   *

I wish there was less emphasis on consumer comment.

I know as much about this church as I want to.
I have not just come in off the street on my way
To the next workhouse, nor has it sprung up overnight.

I probably know more about the congregation
Than the minister does. I live locally.
I could meet them in the shops if I felt inclined.

I long for John Donne, Lancelot Andrewes and Jeremy Taylor
To preach, telling me without consultation
Something I did not realise I ought to know.

I could not bear a hymn in any way associated
With my old mother, my wedding day or my father's death.
Astonish me with an arbitrary song about heaven.

And this strange way of getting offering envelopes.
If I sat here long enough would I end up
With a lapful of them? I prefer Danaean showers.

And about serving the church. If I turned up
With a tin of Brasso and a polisher on Saturday
Would I be held back from using them?

*   *   *

Instead of these rows of dots, filled in by me,
I wish for an articulate commandment about sin.
I wish for a hailstorm of grace.

The Facts of Life

(on reading D.J. Enright's The Terrible Shears)

Rudimentary as light, the facts of life tumble
Down on to a world of trees, each one unique,
Each one a filter, through which a story wriggles.
Over the floor of the forest these stories,
These confessions, stretch out in bright hieroglyphs.

Some of the facts get caught up in the boughs
And itch till Doomsday. Some flutter vividly
And fall to the ground like confetti, single moments
Of a ceremony. The more uneasy the tree
The more eloquent is the pattern it composes.

Poets' minds make the best filters; they deal in fragments.
Their villains never get through the sieve whole.
Even Judas and Pontius Pilate would land piecemeal.
In this book the ungrateful officer Crawford
Arrives as a bite-sized anecdote about biscuits.

In it, too, death has no context. Men fall dead
Off bridges and at railway stations with no word
Of afterwards or before. The disappearance
Of a baby oozes in drops of undrunk milk.
That is childhood, grief in the middle of nothing.

Facts come through the leaves with no judgement of their own.
Like light they kill or cure regardless. They are selected.
They are rejected too and the veto is absolute.
In one golden patch the shadow of a terrible leaf
Has raised its hand and spread its fingers to say 'Halt'.

Coleridge at Ottery St Mary

(for Stephen Spender's birthday)

The grass grew long under the north wall of the churchyard.
Southerly gales whisked it up into waves
And the crows kept vanishing into it and re-appearing
Like black boats. Seaweed washed over the graves.

Here he grew up, a lane and a wall away
From his unappreciative family
And the other villagers. Here a child could dance.
The bells in the tower rang right down to the sea.

The church was a long vessel. He often went on board.
Inside, two Grandissons lay on the ground
Each one telling the time like a sundial:
Their sharp noses moved as the sun came round.

Up under the roof hung the mechanical clock,
Centuries old, with the earth in its old place,
And round it slid the sun, the moon and one star,
Gold as mimosa on the clock's blue face.

Now on winter evenings the clock sounds sick
But then, in a child's daylight it was stronger
Than himself and clanking like a hero. It was part of a poem
To be written when he lived here no longer.

For he took the church and the churchyard away with him
To sea, in a story where sailors lay on a deck
Dead as Grandissons, and the one survivor
Carried a torque of feathers around his neck.

Its heavy muscles pulled his head downwards
But he looked up at the night sky
And saw gold moving competent as clockwork:
The rising moon and the single star of Ottery.

Bright Boy

Stone suits him. He never made
Gestures even while preaching
Out of doors at St Paul's Cross,
And the sounds of oars reaching
Up from the river was loud
Compared with his inert voice.

In front of the cathedral
He sits. Once as a bright boy
He had patrons, became sage,
And now he reads night and day
Fixed in a death-long act of will,
Stone finger clamped to stone page.

His learning provokes the young.
They spray him with misspelt words,
Daub him with garish paint, which
Then gets spread about by birds.
No statue has such scorn flung
At it, so much hate, as his.

If caught, the miscreants have
To scrub him. For an hour
Or so his white curled beard looks
Like a sheep upon his ruff
Till, slopping tins of colour,
They are back. To learn him. *Books*.

The Night Marlowe Died

Christopher Marlowe was a spy, it seems.
His day of pleasure by the River Thames
Should have brought him a handshake and a watch
For faithful service. He had done as much
For anyone who paid him and so had
His three companions. They were really good.

In those days spying was expertly done.
Informers took each other's washing in.
Double agents cancelled themselves out.
Spying had paid for all the wine and meat
Which filled the little room that day in spring
When Marlowe met a different reckoning.

He had been his usual snorting, railing
Blasphemous self, but loyal to his calling,
As they all had to be, to live so well.
He sang a noisy song before he fell,
A dagger stuck in his eye after the feast
As though the Cross had got to him at last.

They saw each other home after his death.
The rats had tired, the streets were out of breath.
Somewhere asleep, the top spymasters lay
Unpicking webs that they had spun by day.
Somewhere, across a park, a peacock's cries
Bewailed the pointlessness of murdering spies.

Wessex Calendar

Stourhead

Happy New Year to all our ancestors,
The rich ones (you) who made the lake, and me
Who called a remote gardener to his tea.
Mine have all died back and so have yours.

We are the wintry paying sightseers
Whose home is somewhere else and who
Live comfortably on salary and fee
And like this place. Nothing above ground stirs.

Lichen has stopped climbing round the urn.
The mole-hills look extinct. The temples crouch
But will not now scuttle away. A turn

In the path brings us full circle through the plans
Of those improvers, and in the last reach
Shine one still light and seven motionless swans.

Dyrham Park

Travellers on the Bath road, jolting south,
Used to listen out for a waterfall,
This à-la-mode cataract, less than a mile
To the next inn. Out of sight underneath

The ridge, it boomed. It had a mouth
Like battle getting nearer. Today all
Is quiet. Nothing but grass pours down the hill.
Fashion translated water into earth

And now there is no way that travellers
Can hear their whereabouts. Yet long before
The cataract was stifled, nearing home

They would have had intimations once a year
Of the perpetual silences to come
For every February this water froze.

Lacock Abbey

Fox-Talbot the photographer lived here.
It seems he was as numerate as God.
At any point on any lane he could
Say how many miles altogether

He had travelled since birth. Each stair
Of the house, each nun and speculator dead,
Clicked on the abacus inside his head.
Deity, poet and photographer

Count differently. God might see the world
As though it were a fountain in the light
Falling in sparrows, rising up in souls.

The poet turns a corner, sees gold curled
Around a lake in March and at first sight
Registers ten thousand daffodils.

Woods Near Alfoxden

Walking in the Quantocks with at least
One poet by her side, she always chose
The woods. In leafless months she heard the noise
Of the sea streaming through. In nights of frost

She spoke familiarly as though she guessed
Rightly the shapes and sizes of the stars.
Under the oaks she saw the holly trees
Hit by the raindrops of a storm long past.

The poets recorded winter on the run
And documented April, but for her
They were the woods in spring. She walked each day

With them even if they were not there.
All three noticed the same leaf, and they
Wrote several lines about it. She wrote one.

Clouds Hill

In those days it was every schoolboy's dream
To become A of B or X of Y,
And to be with some god like Allenby
When he marched into Jerusalem.

This house is small, the garden wet and tame
And he was Lawrence of Arabia
Who received most unwarlike company,
No more the Henty lad who made his name

Blowing up other people's trains. That day
When silence closed in on the final stutters
Of his Brough, he must have come indoors

Where he still manifestly is, the May
Sun picking at the lintel which still bears
The adage roughly translated 'Nothing matters'.

Admiral Hardy's Monument

He should be up there, with the midsummer wind
Mumbling, and then when the southwesters come.
Base, capital and shaft look wrong without him.
There is no doubt which way he would have turned

When hoisted up, above the shallow land
And hedges shaped like waves but twice as warm.
He would have faced the canvas and the foam
That led back to Trafalgar and beyond,

As did his sappy memories. He grew
Ripe with stories in his admiral's praise
And was still telling one before he died:

'By God, I'll not lose Hardy.' Nelson cried
'Back the mizzen topsail.' We all have days
Like that, especially looking out to sea.

Assembly Rooms, Bath

On this hot dusty day the Assembly Rooms
Sweat under plastic sheets. Through a crack
I see men re-creating plasterwork.
I have no right to peer. Somebody comes

Out to defend the mystery of tombs
For restoration goes on in them. Hark
At the gallants and gamesters coming back.
I hear the rhythm of those piping times.

The building will reappear like Lazarus
Though in no special season. Blackbeetle chairs
Will not cluster round the Pump Room (now

The Treatment Centre and you go by bus).
Somebody will be showing to visitors
The grave clothes of two hundred years ago.

Langdon Hill

Half-way up, a path goes round the hill,
An iron band circling a barrel. One
Farmer cutting corn lowers the skyline.
One distant sheep sprawls like a last petal.

Foxgloves and heather congregate in purple
And butterflies open and shut again
Their illuminated pages in the sun.
Up from the valley sounds a bugle-call.

This summons from the tents that stand down there
Like corn-stooks in the Bible, prophesying,
Comes now to paramilitary boys.

Vespasian was here, and winked to war
The Second Legion. And here some of those
Still are, who saw this hill as they were dying.

Nailsea Glass

In England in September people go
Indoors, to paintings, glass and porcelain,
Their own or some museum's. Nailsea men
Who worked in glass were much less comme-il-faut

And Christian than their kind but they could blow
Glass better and they threw a crystal chain
Of objects round the world and back again.
In galleries and at auctions they still glow.

Nailsea do-gooders founded Sunday Schools.
The blowers had their own theology
And called the furnaces Hell Mouth. The flames

That led to drunkenness and nudity
Ended as cool green glass. Their hands and names
Were black, their wares bright as saved souls.

Brent Knoll

Down in the valley clergymen who smelled
Of damp cloth and of well-used handkerchieves
Wrote aggrieved poetry about the waves
That fenced the church, the clapped-out bell that tolled

For the parishioners who died of cold
And fog, and splashed into their graves
Even in October when the leaves
Fell and floated in a scum of gold.

Today is frivolous. Down there the wet
Noses of the cattle sparkle across Sedgemoor.
So does the motorway, rackety and bright

As a day at the races. And up here
The long dead whistle towards us, seeming to bring
Iron Age high spirits, if there was such a thing.

Bruton Dovecot

If the monks really kept doves here
In this tower which was the Abbot's last
Improvement (then the Protestants came west)
Today would be like the doves' ancient terror:

The cattle killed and salted, quiet November,
Fresh blood in the sky turning to rust,
Cold dung stiffening from rain to frost
And men with nets walking up to the tower.

They went inside shutting the door. And though
A darkness of birds thundered towards the light
Each net came down again with a dead weight

Of life and fear and feathers. The dovecot,
If that is what it was, has no roof now
Yet stares like a death cell into Somerset.

Thomas Hardy's Birthplace

When the Dear Memory, as his widow spoke
Of him, remembered in old age his place
Of birth, he called it rambling, though a house
With seven rooms cannot wander far. His talk

Of all their Christmas dancing was more like
The truth. The guests, to whom he would refer
As being of substantial footing, were.
They pounded up the lamplight and the smoke.

Only the fingerprints of Egdon Heath
Survive. Winter returns, complete as new.
The clouds hang down and move like long skirts dancing

Out of sight one by one. The cat glancing
Into the parlour might have had such a view
As he went outside to apportion death.

Observations

At the Airport

Five wet aeroplanes on the tarmac.
The rain has just stopped.

Outside the departure lounge
A yellow puddle lies cold and still.

Into it as I look down
Comes an aeroplane,
Still high but homing,
Its struggles above the Atlantic
Nearly over.

It takes its place in the water

A fly in amber.

Outside Athens

On the Boetian plain
RECKITT AND COLMAN stand akimbo.
To the left olive trees bustle uphill.

Possession is something
The guide cannot get the English hang of:
Over there took place some of the Apostles' Acts,
Up there the complex of Oedipus.

Sunflowers

Driving from Xanthi to Kavalla
One holiday morning
We come face to face
With a field of sunflowers.

They stare into the Aegean sun
As we cannot.

Coming back that evening
After a millennium of ruins
And ghosts that thrive in heat
We face the flowers again.
Like ourselves they have turned round,

Double-dyed, everlasting bystanders
Gaping from dawn to dark
From east to west

Ready to see Alexander
March over the hills
From this direction or that,

Or any other army.

Houses in Holland

Two old houses on the canal
Share a wall, share dust
But are not aligned
Like Siamese twins.
They live at different levels.

As I go up the stairs of this one,
A thin wall at my side,
Footsteps shuffle through my hair,
Somebody sings at angel height,
My bent knee coughs.

Storm

White birds are coming up the valley
Fifteen miles from the sea.
There will be a storm.

They gather by the river
Like saved souls relaxing
But do not seem to believe it.
They start up as restlessly
As hot oil spitting
And fall back into the same spot.

We have purposeful things to do
Before the storm catches us all.
It is shouting in the distance already
And the clouds have started to run.

The birds have frightened us
With their white annunciation.

We are used to black birds.

February

Our lane is a museum
Sheets of ice cover marvellous exhibits.

Here is a man's hand
Made out of twigs brown as blood.

The man is gone.
His bones have gone and his flesh.
His veins beckon through the glass.
My foot slips.

From the Cliff

Northwards.
Twenty young men on bicycles
Swim along the lane.
The hedge comes up to their handlebars
A tree rises to cover them
A gate dips to reveal them
Their backs are curved
They gleam like fish.

Southwards.
A score of dolphins
Leap for nobody but the Lord.
They arch over the sea like cyclists
They shine like machinery.

Worm-Charming at Easter

You must not break the turf,
Certainly not dig.
You can make an earthquake
With the prongs of a large fork.
You can bring a pony to stamp.
You can play a trombone.

Underground together for an age
The worms rise to their summit meeting
Individual as statesmen.

After the competing and the counting
They will go down to their joint darkness again
Away from the sharp birds and the pink hands
Which will follow.

Birthday

Four candles at face level,
My aunt down on her hunkers
Showing me my cake;

A cow's eyes in the headlamps
Of the only car
That went down our lane.

I blew them all into the dark.